STAR ★ FILES

Andre Benjamin

Brian Fitzgerald

www.raintreepublishers.co.uk
Visit our website to find out more information about **Raintree** books.

To order:
☎ Phone 44 (0) 1865 888113
📄 Send a fax to 44 (0) 1865 314091
💻 Visit the Raintree Bookshop at **www.raintreepublishers.co.uk** to browse our catalogue and order online.

(handwritten: 428.64 FIT)

Produced for Raintree by
White-Thomson Publishing Ltd
Bridgewater Business Centre
210 High Street, Lewes, BN7 2NH

First published in Great Britain by Raintree,
Halley Court, Jordan Hill, Oxford OX2 8EJ,
part of Harcourt Education.
Raintree is a registered trademark
of Harcourt Education Ltd.

Editorial: Nicola Hodgson and Adam Miller
Design: Tinstar Design Ltd (www.tinstar.co.uk)
and Michelle Lisseter
Picture Research: Nicola Hodgson
Production: Chloe Bloom

Originated by Modern Age
Printed and bound in China by
South China Printing Company

Paperback   Hardback
ISBN 1 844 43973 9   ISBN 1 844 43972 0
ISBN 978 1 844 43973 7   ISBN 978 1 844 43972 0
10 09 08 07 06   09 08 07 06 05
10 9 8 7 6 5 4 3 2 1   10 9 8 7 6 5 4 3 2 1

**British Library Cataloguing in
Publication Data**
Fitzgerald, Brian.
Andre Benjamin. – (Star Files)
782.4' 21649' 092
A full catalogue record for this book
is available from the British Library.

Acknowledgements
The publishers would like to thank the following
for permission to reproduce photographs: Corbis
pp. **11** (l) (Tim Mosenfelder), **14** (r), **22** (Tim
Mosenfelder), **31** (Mike Blake), **40** (Melanie
Burford); Getty Images pp. **4**, **6** (b), **21** (Frank
Micelotta), **25** (Kevin Winter), **26** (b) (Frank
Micelotta), **27** (l), **32** (Giulio Marcocchi);
Retna Pictures pp. **6** (t) (Howard Denner), **8** (l)
(Richard Reyes), **9** (Sara De Boer), **11** (r) (Scott D.
Smith), **12** (b) (Ernie Paniccioli), **15** (b) (John
Halpern), **16**, **18** (Lillian Bonomo), **19** (r)
(Edward Dougherty), **20** (Elgin Edmonds), **23**
(Kelly A. Swift), **29** (King Collection), **33** (t)
(Robb D. Cohen), **35** (l) (Lillian Bonomo), **35** (r)
(Michael Layton); Rex Features pp. **5** (LXL), **7**
(James McCauley), **8** (r) (Dave Allocca), **10** (Joyce
Silverstein), **12** (t) (Richard Young), **13** (Erik
Pendzich), **14** (l) (Sipa Press), **15** (t) (John Carver),
17 (t) (Brian Rasic), **17** (b) (Everett Collection),
19 (l) (Munawar Hosain), **24** (Marco Dos Santos),
26 (t) (Dan Steinberg), **27** (r) (Everett Collection),
28 (l) (Matt Baron), **28** (r) (Everett Collection),
30 (Alex Maguire), **34** (Everett Collection),
36 (MGM/Everett), **37** (Bill Zygmant), **38**
(John Taylor), **39** (Everett Collection), **41**
(Peter Brooker), **42** (Bill Davila), **43** (Brian Rasic).
Cover photograph reproduced with permission
of Getty Images.

Quote sources: p. **5** www.hiphopdx.com,
24 September 2003; p. **7** *People*, 16 February
2004; pp. **9**, **43** (b) mtv.com, 14 October 2003;
p. **10** *Jet*, 2 February 2004; pp. **13**, **25** (l)
Entertainment Weekly, 10 November 2003; p. **15**
Hey Ya! The Unauthorized Biography of Outkast,
Chris Nickson, St. Martin's Griffin, 2004; p. **16**
Rolling Stone, 23 November 2000; p. **18** mtv.com,
6 November 2000; p. **23** mtv.com, 14 October
2000; p. **25** (r) *Spin*, March 2001; p. **27** *Rolling
Stone*, 13 November 2003; pp. **28**, **43** (t) *Blender*,
April 2004; pp. **32**, **33** *Time*, 29 September 2003;
p. **38** *Esquire*, September 2004; pp. **40**, **41**
mtv.com, 7 September 2004.

The publishers would like to thank Sarah
Williams, Charly Rimsa, Catherine Clarke,
and Caroline Hamilton for their assistance
in the preparation of this book.

Contents

Any words appearing in the text in bold, **like this**, are explained in the glossary. You can also look out for them in the "Star Words" box at the bottom of each page.

Andre's world

ALL ABOUT ANDRE

Full Name: Andre Benjamin (also known as Dre or Andre 3000)
Born: May 27, 1975
Place of birth: Atlanta, Georgia
Family: Sharon Benjamin-Hodo (mother), Lawrence Walker (father)
Children: Seven Sirius (son)
Height: 1.83 metres (6 feet)
Big break: Meeting record producer Rico Wade
First album: *Southernplayalisticadillacmuzik*
Other interests: acting, painting, designing clothes

The music world is full of very special and very talented people. Andre Benjamin really is one of a kind, though. He is very different from many other people in music. He does not drink alcohol or use drugs. His songs have a positive message. Andre, often called Dre for short, is known for his wild style of dress. He is also a vegetarian. Andre does not follow trends – he sets them.

Perfect pair

Andre and his music partner Antwan "Big Boi" Patton have made Outkast the most popular hip-hop group in the world. The group draws from a wide range of **influences**, including rock, jazz, R&B, and the **blues**.

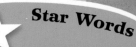

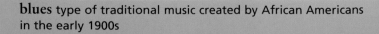

Star Words

blues type of traditional music created by African Americans in the early 1900s

Andre and Big Boi love to take risks with their music. They always try to create songs that sound different from anything else. Their fans love the results. Outkast has sold millions of albums and has won a lot of awards.

> **I like being an individual in my dress and in my music.**

Andre enjoys looking for new challenges. He is more than just a musician. He is also an actor, artist, **producer**, and clothing designer. Andre just might be able to do anything he sets his mind to!

Andre shows off his style at the 2004 MTV Europe Music Awards.

Find out later

What year did the first Outkast album come out?

Who is one of Andre's musical heroes?

What movie did Andre act in with Uma Thurman?

producer music producers decide how a song will sound when it is being recorded

Early life

Andre was an only child. His parents split when he was young. He was raised in a single-parent home. Andre's mother, Sharon, worked hard to give him a good life. She and Andre moved around a lot because she could not always afford to pay their rent.

Andre grew up in a rough part of Atlanta, Georgia, USA. The schools were not very good there. Sharon wanted something better for her son. She put Andre into a program that took kids to better schools in white neighbourhoods.

Atlanta is one of the largest US cities. More than 4 million people live there.

Georgia born

Several soul music legends are from Georgia, like Andre. Otis Redding and James Brown (above), known as "the Godfather of Soul", started their careers in Macon, Georgia. Ray Charles, from Albany, made the song "Georgia on My Mind" a classic.

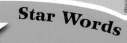

New world

Andre's new school was like another world. He became interested in things that most other African-American kids did not know about. These things included skateboarding and rock music. Andre could not afford the expensive designer clothes that his classmates wore. He sewed his own labels onto his shirts instead.

★ Star fact

Andre did not always want to be a music star. "I thought I'd be an architect," he said, "but I didn't like maths."

Big change

Andre started to **rebel** when he entered high school near home. His grades slipped and he began to get into trouble in and out of school. When Andre was fifteen, Sharon sent him to live with his father. Andre enrolled in Tri-Cities High School. He had decided that he wanted to become a rapper, and Tri-Cities had a very good **performing arts** program. There, he met a classmate who would change his life.

Get to know Andre

Favourite food:
Broccoli

Least favourite food:
Aubergine

Favourite pastime:
Listening to music

Least favourite pastime:
Business meetings

Favourite city to visit:
Los Angeles

In April 2004, Andre was given a special Heroes Award by his hometown of Atlanta.

rebel act against people in charge

Music men

Andre and Big Boi both liked rap music that was creative and had a positive message by groups such as De La Soul (below). They were also fans of music legends such as James Brown and Jimi Hendrix.

Big Boi on campus

Antwan Patton began attending Tri-Cities High School at the same time as Andre. He had recently moved to Atlanta to live with his aunt. Antwan was short, but he had a big attitude. His friends began calling him "Big Boi" as a joke, and the nickname stuck.

Andre and Big Boi's love of crazy clothes is one of the many things that helped them become friends.

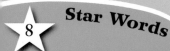

Star Words   argyle pattern with diamond shapes

Big Boi was born in Savannah, Georgia, USA. He was the oldest of five children. Fifteen people, including Big Boi's cousins, all lived in a small three-bedroom house. When he was a kid, Big Boi usually had to share a bed with at least one other person.

Friends and outcasts

Andre and Big Boi first met at a local shopping centre. The boys became friends. They soon realized that they had a lot in common. One of the main things that brought them together was that they were so different from everyone else. Big Boi and Andre had their own **unique** style of dress. They dressed like rich white kids with smart shoes, **argyle** socks, and V-neck sweaters. They also created new styles to set them apart even further.

Crazy clothes

Big Boi remembers some of the crazy fashion ideas he and Andre came up with: "We would cut our clothes up and dye them different colours … just so people at school would say, 'Damn, where'd you get that?'" Today, they are still known for their wild clothes.

One of gangsta rap's biggest stars, Ice Cube is now also a famous actor.

unique different from everything else

Dynamic duo

Organized Noize

The three members of Organized Noize are Rico Wade, Raymon Murray, and Pat "Sleepy" Brown. The trio had their biggest success working with TLC on the hit single "Waterfalls". It was the No. 1 single of 1994.

Andre and Big Boi began to practice their rapping skills. They staged rap battles in the cafeteria at school. One day they were watching music videos at Big Boi's house. The boys thought that they were just as good as the rappers on television. They decided to start their own group.

The perfect name

The boys' original name was 2 Shades Deep, but it did not fit. They wanted a name to match their part as outsiders. They looked in a dictionary and found the perfect name. "We came across the word 'outcast' and just kept the **pronunciation key** spelling of it," Andre remembered. Outkast was born.

TLC is one of the top female R&B groups of all time.

Star Words

audition interview for a musician or actor, where they show their skills

Tough choice

Andre always had a hard time with his studies. He decided to drop out of school to spend more time on his rap **career**. Andre knew education was important, however. He went back later and earned his **diploma.** Big Boi wanted to become a star too, but he was also a good student. He stayed in school and graduated with good marks.

Andre and Big Boi got a big break when they met **producer** Rico Wade. Wade was from a group named Organized Noize. The boys did an **audition** for Wade in a parking lot. He really liked what he heard. Wade took them to his basement music studio, which was called the Dungeon. Andre and Big Boi spent many days in the studio, writing songs and waiting for their big chance.

Ludacris toured with Outkast in 2001.

Atlanta rappers

Before Outkast, most rap stars came from New York or Los Angeles. Outkast helped make Atlanta a major city in the rap world. Ludacris and Lil Jon and the East Side Boyz are just two of the many rap acts from Atlanta.

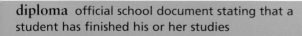

Andre and Big Boi improved their rap skills by practicing whenever they could.

diploma official school document stating that a student has finished his or her studies

Face the music

After months of hard work, Outkast got an **audition** with LaFace Records. The name LaFace combines the nicknames of its two founders, Antonio "L. A." Reid and Kenneth "Babyface" Edmonds.

L. A. Reid liked what he heard. He wanted to sign Andre and Big Boi to a **recording contract**. He had to wait a few months, however. The boys' parents would not let them sign the contract until they were eighteen.

Some of LaFace's top acts include:
- Usher (above): His hits include "You Make Me Wanna" and "Yeah".
- TLC: Their album *CrazySexyCool* sold more than 11 million copies.
- Toni Braxton: She had a huge hit in 1996 with "Unbreak My Heart".

Andre and Big Boi were still teenagers when they had their first hit.

Star Words

recording contract agreement between an artist and a record label to make music together

Everyday people

Outkast's first song came out in 1993. It was called "Player's Ball". It was different to a lot of other rap songs of the time. Andre and Big Boi did not rap about having a lot of money and expensive cars. "Player's Ball" talked about everyday life in the poor neighbourhoods near Atlanta. The song featured Andre singing the chorus in a high voice. This was also very unusual for a rap song.

Sean Combs is also known as P. Diddy.

"Player's Ball" became a big hit. Andre used his first cheque from writing the song to buy a 1990 Cadillac. He would soon have a lot more cheques to cash. Outkast released their first album in April 1994. It had one of the craziest titles ever; *Southernplayalisticadillacmuzik*. The album went platinum. This means it sold more than 1 million copies.

⭐ Star fact

L. A. Reid explains why he thinks Outkast are so great. "They've never tried to be hip or current or now. They've always been very original. That's what keeps me excited."

"Player's Ball" caught the attention of a lot of people in music. One of them was Sean "Puffy" Combs. He asked to direct the music video for the song. Within a couple of years, Sean would become a major rap star too.

Fresh start

After the success of Outkast's first album, Andre decided to change his lifestyle. He wanted to live more healthily, so he gave up smoking and drinking alcohol. He also became a strict vegetarian. Andre is so concerned with his health that he will not even chew gum!

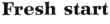
Andre likes to eat healthy foods.

Sexiest vegetarian

In 2004, Andre was voted the sexiest male vegetarian in an online poll. The female winner was Alicia Silverstone (above), the star of the movie *Clueless*. Past winners include Tobey Maguire, Natalie Portman, and Shania Twain.

Andre's clothes also became more **outrageous**. On a trip to Jamaica he decided to grow out his **dreadlocks.** He wanted to keep his hair covered while it grew, so he began to wear a **turban.** Soon after that he began to wear silk scarves and other colourful clothes. People thought he was going crazy!

⭐ Star fact

Andre cannot stand being around cigarette smoke. Sometimes he will leave clubs or parties early just to get away from the smell.

Star Words   dreadlocks long thin mats of hair that have been allowed to grow out over a long period of time without being combed

Out of this world

Andre and Big Boi's next album was like nothing anyone had heard before. Some people said the music sounded like it was from outer space! The title, *ATLiens*, combined their home Atlanta with the word aliens. "Being an alien is just being yourself when people don't understand you," Andre explained.

For *ATLiens*, Andre and Big Boi used live musicians in the studio instead of recorded music or **samples.** This was very rare for a rap album at the time. Fans liked what they heard. *ATLiens* was released in 1996. It became Outkast's second straight platinum album.

Outkast's second album was even more successful than their first.

★ ★ ★ ★ ★ ★ ★

Funky sounds

The space-age sound of *ATLiens* reminded a lot of people of the music of George Clinton (above) and his bands Parliament and Funkadelic. He was a huge star in the 1970s. Like Andre, Clinton is known for his wild outfits and funky music.

★ ★ ★ ★ ★ ★ ★ ★ ★

sample part of a recording that is used by another artist to create a new song

15

Crazy clothes

Rico Wade of Organized Noize says of Andre's crazy clothes: "I remember him saying, 'I just want to look like the music, man, as funky and as exciting as the music. Why should the music sound better than I look?'"

Written in the stars

Outkast called their next album *Aquemini*. This album came out in 1998. The name combined the guys' star signs. Big Boi is an Aquarius and Andre is a Gemini. It showed that they were very different people, but they came together to form one great team.

For the first time, Andre and Big Boi produced many of the songs on the album. Like their previous albums, *Aquemini* avoided using a lot of rap **clichés**. Andre and Big Boi did not promote violence or boast about their wealth. Their lyrics had a positive message and showed that they were responsible adults.

Andre sometimes dresses like he's from another planet!

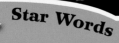

Star Words   civil rights movement struggle of African Americans in the 1950s and 1960s to gain the same rights as white people

Get on the bus

The biggest hit from the album was "Rosa Parks". It was meant to be a **tribute**, but it got Outkast into trouble. Rosa Parks was a great figure in the **civil rights movement**. In the 1950s, US buses were **segregated**. White people sat in the front, and African Americans sat in the back. In December 1955, Rosa Parks refused to give up her bus seat to a white man. She was thrown in jail. This made people **boycott** the buses in her hometown of Montgomery, Alabama. This was the first great protest of the civil rights movement.

Rosa did not like Outkast using her name without permission. She sued the group and LaFace – even though the song was not really about her at all.

⭐ Star fact

Robert Hodo, the pastor at Andre's church, played harmonica on "Rosa Parks".

Lauryn Hill

After *Aquemini* was released, Outkast went on tour with Lauryn Hill (above). She is a talented singer and rapper from the popular group the Fugees. Her first solo album, *The Miseducation of Lauryn Hill*, was the top album of 1998.

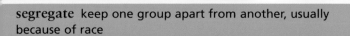

Rosa Parks is a hero to many African Americans, including Outkast.

segregate keep one group apart from another, usually because of race

Aquemini was another huge success. It sold more than 2 million copies. In 2000 Andre and Big Boi started their own record label. They named it after their hit album. They wanted to give new artists a chance – just as LaFace had done for them. One of the first artists they signed was Killer Mike. His **debut** album, *Monster*, reached the top ten on the US album chart in 2003.

Stankonia

Andre explained that Stankonia was a made-up magical place. "We want to bring the people to this free, funky place," he said, "where all the energies it takes to make this music come from." Andre's outfits became even wilder around this time. He wore platinum wigs, feather boas, and ski boots. He also announced that his new name was Andre 3000.

New studio

Andre and Big Boi also bought a recording studio and named it Stankonia. R.E.M. and Whitney Houston are two of the many artists who have recorded there. The strange name also became the title of Outkast's next album.

Only Andre would dare to wear this crazy outfit!

Star Words   debut first

Big Boi wears an old New York Mets baseball shirt.

Outkast took home their first Grammy award in 2002.

Making magic

The album *Stankonia* came out in 2000. It was their biggest hit to that point. The single "Ms. Jackson" became Outkast's first song to top the US Billboard charts. *Stankonia* won the Grammy for Best Rap Album. "Ms. Jackson" earned Andre and Big Boi another Grammy for Best Rap Performance by a Duo or Group.

Big Boi style

Big Boi also began a fashion trend. He was the first rapper to wear "throwback" sports shirts. These are uniforms that are no longer worn by football, baseball, and basketball teams because the logos have changed. Soon, almost every rapper was wearing these shirts.

Erykah Badu

Andre and Erykah Badu have a lot in common. She is also a vegetarian and is known for wearing **turbans**. Like Andre, she is a talented singer who has appeared in movies. Her first album, *Baduizm*, won a Grammy for best R&B album in 1997.

Young love

Andre's own life was the **inspiration** for the song "Ms. Jackson". Several years earlier, he met singer Erykah Badu and fell in love. The couple had a son who was born in November 1996. They named him Seven Sirius.

Andre and Erykah grew apart. He lived in Atlanta and she and Seven lived in Dallas, Texas, more than 1100 kilometres (700 miles) away. In 2000 Andre and Erykah split up. They are still very close friends.

Seven was born in Erykah Badu's home in November 1996.

Star Words   inspiration idea that you get from people or things

Musical promise

"Ms. Jackson" is written to the grandmother of the singer's baby. He promises that he will always be there for his son even though he has split up with the baby's mother. With the song, Andre and Big Boi showed that they were committed to their kids. This is not a very common **theme** in rap music.

Andre's own father was not around for much of his childhood. Andre did not make the same mistake with his own son. Even though they live very far away from each other, Andre visits Seven as often as he can. He also brought him to the 2004 Grammy Awards.

★ ★ ★ ★ ★ ★ ★ ★ ★

Big Boi's kids

Big Boi also has kids. He has a daughter, Jordan, and two sons, Bamboo and Cross. Big Boi is just like any other dad. Other parents could not believe it when he showed up at his kids' football games and cheered along with everyone else.

★ ★ ★ ★ ★ ★ ★ ★ ★

Andre brought Seven onstage with him to accept one of his 2004 Grammy Awards.

theme topic or subject

A new era

★ ★ ★ ★ ★ ★ ★ ★

Two buses

Andre and Big
Boi had separate
$1 million tour
buses. Big Boi's
bus had a lot of
people, parties,
and loud music.
Andre's bus was
just the opposite.
It was so quiet
that it was called
"the church bus".

★ ★ ★ ★ ★ ★ ★ ★

With *Stankonia*, Outkast had finally moved into
mainstream music. They appealed to fans of all
types of music, not just hip-hop. When they
went out on tour they noticed that much of
their audience was white.

Crazy concerts

Outkast's Stank Love tour of 2001 was like no
other rap concert. Most rap acts stood on an
empty stage with only a DJ behind them.
Outkast's stage set looked like a cave on the
moon. The duo was backed up by a full band.
Andre and Big Boi were full of energy, and the
crowds loved it.

Outkast spent most of 2001
playing sold-out shows.

Star Words   mainstream what appeals to most people

Giving back

While on tour, Andre and Big Boi teamed up with the Nike Youth Action program. Violence in schools was becoming a big problem in the United States. This program aimed to make kids unafraid to speak up and prevent violence in schools. Andre and Big Boi talked to kids about school violence. They donated money to children's groups. They also gave free concert tickets to many of the kids they spoke to.

Andre's mix tape

Andre's ultimate mix tape would include songs by these artists:

- John Coltrane
- The Smiths
- Prince
- 2 Live Crew
- The Hives
- Funkadelic

" I want everybody in the world to get a chance to listen to my music. "

Best of the bunch

In the summer of 2001, Outkast toured the United States with the Area: One Tour. This tour brought together artists from different musical styles. Other acts included rockers Incubus, pop singer Nelly Furtado, and dance-music wizard Moby. In every city, the crowds loved Outkast the best.

"Howlin'" Pelle Almqvist of Swedish rockers The Hives.

Funky fresh

The *Stankonia* album and tour brought Outkast thousands of new fans. Many of these new fans did not know most of the group's earlier songs. For their next album, Outkast released a collection of their biggest hits. The album came out just in time for Christmas 2001. It was named *Big Boi & Dre Present . . . Outkast.*

All of their hits were included, beginning with "Player's Ball". Fans got to hear the songs that helped Outkast change hip-hop music. They heard how Andre and Big Boi brought different styles of music together to make some great songs. Like Outkast's first three albums, this one went platinum.

★ Star fact

In March 2002 Andre and Big Boi won a World Music Award as the best-selling rap group in the entire world.

★★★★★★★★
Soundtracks

Andre and Big Boi's songs have appeared on many movie **soundtracks**. This is a good way to reach new fans. Outkast's music was included in the films *Soul Food* (1997), *Tomb Raider* (2001), and *Scooby-Doo* (2002).

★★★★★★★★

Outkast were on top of the rap world in 2002.

Star Words   soundtrack music used in a movie

Outkast accept their Grammy award in 2002.

The Whole World

Big Boi & Dre Present . . . Outkast did not just contain old songs. The album included three tracks that fans had not heard before. One of them was "The Whole World". This song is about keeping a positive outlook even when things are going badly.

The song featured a rap by Killer Mike. "The Whole World" earned Andre and Big Boi their second Grammy for Best Rap Performance by a Duo or Group.

> We wanted to shock the hip-hip community, anybody who listens to music . . . We wanted to revive it.

Outkast fans

Andre says that there is no such thing as a typical Outkast fan. "Your mum might be an Outkast fan; your little brother might be an Outkast fan; the white guy who likes Led Zeppelin might be an Outkast fan. I think aliens dig us, too."

25

Going solo

After all the group's success, Andre wanted to try something new. He began writing love songs for a movie project. When the film got scrapped, Andre wanted to use the songs on a solo album instead. Big Boi and Outkast's **manager** hated the idea. They came up with another idea: both Big Boi and Andre would create solo albums. The two records would be released as a double Outkast album.

Guest stars

The Love Below was not a completely solo project. Actress Rosario Dawson (above) and singer Norah Jones sang duets with Andre on the album. Big Boi rapped on one of the album's biggest hits, "Roses".

Andre showed off his guitar skills on *The Love Below*.

Star words

deadline due date
instrumental song that does not include any singing

Planning The Love Below

Big Boi worked quickly. He completed his album, called *Speakerboxxx*, by February 2003. Andre's project dragged on and he missed **deadlines.** The album was a very personal one for Andre. He wanted it to be perfect.

Andre was given a final due date: the end of August. In the last days he worked in four studios at once, trying to finish. "I stayed up for four straight days to get it done," he said.

Big finish

It was worth the wait. Andre's album was called *The Love Below*. It was totally unusual – even for him. All of the songs dealt with love. Andre showed that he was more than just a rapper. He was also a talented singer and musician. Andre only rapped on one song. He played keyboards and guitar on the album. He even played saxophone on one song.

Andre plays a lot of instruments, including the saxophone.

My Favourite Things

One of the strangest tracks on *The Love Below* is "My Favourite Things". The song first appeared in the 1965 film *The Sound of Music*. Jazz saxophonist John Coltrane (above) later created a famous **instrumental** version. Andre added a fast techno drumbeat to the song.

manager music managers take care of the business side of a pop star's career

Andre shows off a special "The Love Below" jacket with the help of Farnsworth Bentley, P. Diddy's former assistant.

Hey Ya

The most popular song on *The Love Below* was "Hey Ya". Some people have called it the perfect pop song. Do not be fooled by its catchy beat, though. Andre explains that the song is actually quite sad. He says it is about "how people stay together because **tradition** says they should, even if they're unhappy."

"Hey Ya" was a huge hit. Even rock radio stations played it. It was No. 1 on the US Billboard chart for 9 weeks. For eight of those weeks Big Boi's "The Way You Move" stood right behind it at No. 2. This was the first time since The Beatles in 1964 that the same group held the top two spots for that long.

Long history

The idea for "Hey Ya" was 5 or 6 years old. Andre was just learning to play the guitar at the time. He wanted to create a song that sounded like the famous punk-rock band The Ramones. Andre played all the instruments on the song, except bass.

Star words   tradition usual way of doing things

The "Hey Ya" video was based on early performances by the Beatles.

The video

"Hey Ya" also had a great music video. It was based on The Beatles' first appearance on US television on *The Ed Sullivan Show*.

Like a Polaroid

In "Hey Ya", Andre tells listeners to "shake it like a Polaroid picture." Polaroid cameras print out photos just after you take them. People often shake these pictures to make them dry faster. Shaking a Polaroid can actually damage it, though!

The Ramones were an **inspiration** to Andre.

Eight people

Andre played all eight members of the band in the video "Hey Ya":

- Dookie, the drummer
- Possum Jenkins, the bass player
- Benjamin Andre, the keyboard player
- Johnny Vulture, the guitarist
- Andre (Ice Cold) 3000, the singer
- The Love Haters, the three backing singers

Rap winners

Before Outkast's big win, only four rap albums had ever been **nominated** for album of the year at the Grammys. They are: *Please Hammer Don't Hurt 'Em* by MC Hammer (1990); *The Marshall Mathers LP* (2000), and *The Eminem Show* (2002) by Eminem; and Outkast's own *Stankonia* (2001).

Double success

"Hey Ya" helped make *Speakerboxxx/The Love Below* the hottest album of the year. Fans did not only love Andre's album. They thought Big Boi's was great, too.

Special guests

Speakerboxxx was the perfect mate for *The Love Below*. It sounded a lot like Outkast's earlier albums, but it was even better. Some of the biggest names in rap music, including Jay-Z and Ludacris, appeared on *Speakerboxxx*.

Sleepy Brown from Organized Noize joined Big Boi on the huge hit "The Way You Move".

Speakerboxxx/The Love Below was the first Outkast album to reach No. 1 on the Billboard chart. It was in the top spot for 7 weeks. The album sold 3 million copies in its first month alone!

Eminem has won the Grammy for best rap album three times.

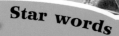

Diamond status

In the 1990s the record industry created a **category** that was even higher than platinum. Any album that sold more than 10 million copies reached diamond status. *Speakerboxxx/The Love Below* hit the diamond mark in December 2004.

Big winners

Speakerboxxx/The Love Below also won many awards. Andre and Big Boi won three awards at the 2004 Grammys. One of them was the highest honour: best album of the year. Outkast became the first hip-hop group ever to win that award. Outkast also won four MTV Video Music Awards, including best video of the year for "Hey Ya".

Grammy win

Andre and Big Boi celebrated their Grammy win with a huge party at a mansion in Hollywood, California. They served some favourite south American foods, such as spare ribs, cornbread, and macaroni and cheese. Guests included Christina Aguilera, Jessica Simpson, and Beck.

Big Boi and Andre celebrate winning three Grammy awards.

Game on!

One of Big Boi's favourite hobbies is playing video games. His favourite game is NFL Football. In February 2004, he played several Outkast fans on Xbox Live over the internet. He beat them all!

Double trouble?

After *Speakerboxxx/The Love Below* came out, **rumours** spread through the **media** that Outkast was splitting up. Many people thought it was strange that Big Boi and Andre recorded full albums without each other. The two rarely gave interviews together. They even lived on different sides of the United States. Big Boi was still in Atlanta, but Andre spent most of his time in Los Angeles.

Still strong

Andre and Big Boi did not care about the rumours. They had been together for more than 10 years. They were as close as brothers. They also knew that Outkast was as strong as ever. Andre and Big Boi just wanted to do different things with their **careers**. As Andre explained, "People got it all wrong. It's about growing up, not breaking up."

Big Boi spends a lot of his free time playing video games.

Star words

downloads files that are copied from the internet onto a computer

Big Boi performed many of Outkast's biggest hits on his 2004 solo tour.

Solo tour

Andre was not interested in going on tour. He said that touring did not excite him anymore. He wanted to spend his time on other projects, like acting. Big Boi did not mind. He went out on tour by himself. He played to sold-out crowds across the United States.

Opposites attract

The two men had always been different. Big Boi often dressed like other rappers. Andre wore whatever he wanted. Big Boi loved loud parties, but Andre was more laid back. Their differences are a big part of what makes them such a great team.

> Our love for each other is greater than our love of music. (Big Boi)

Downloads

In 2004, the record industry gave out its first awards for music sold through internet **downloads**. Three out of the six songs that were downloaded most often were Outkast songs. They were "Hey Ya", "Roses", and "The Way You Move".

media types of communication such as television, radio, internet, newspapers, and magazines

Other interests

Punk'd

Andre and Big Boi appeared on an episode of MTV's *Punk'd*. When the guys leave a party one night, they find their rental car smashed through a shop window. They are shocked when a police officer tells them they owe $350,000 in damages. Then host Ashton Kutcher shows up to tell them it is just a joke.

Andre has many interests outside Outkast. He takes clarinet and saxophone lessons. He has even taken tap-dancing lessons to be like Sammy Davis, Jr., one of his heroes. Sammy Davis, Jr. was one of the first African American entertainers to be equally popular with white and black audiences. Like Andre, he had many talents. He was a musician, singer, actor, and dancer.

Paint job

Andre has been a painter since he was young. His paintings are very bold and colourful. They are almost **surreal** – just like his music. An advertisement for his paintings appeared on the booklet for the *Speakerboxxx/The Love Below* CD. Andre's talent as an artist led him to make a deal with the Cartoon Network. He wants to create a show about his Johnny Vulture character from the "Hey Ya" video.

Like Andre, Sammy Davis, Jr., was one of the coolest performers of his time.

Star fact

Andre is friends with actress Sharon Stone. He arrived at her birthday party in March 2004 with a special gift: a plate of homemade chocolate chip cookies!

Star words   inducted admitted as a member

Back to school?

Andre tries to be a well-rounded person. He wishes that he had some formal training in music. He has said that he would like to study classical music at the Juilliard School of Music in New York. This is the top music school in the United States. He has also said that he would like to attend Oxford University.

Andre has also produced songs for other artists. He wrote and produced the songs "Long Way to Go" and "Bubble Pop" for the first solo album by No Doubt singer Gwen Stefani. Gwen said that she was nervous about working with Andre because he is so talented.

Andre's hero

Legendary musician Prince (above) has always been one of Andre's heroes because of his **unique** style. In March 2004, Andre got one of the biggest thrills of his life. He **inducted** Prince into the Rock and Roll Hall of Fame.

Andre worked on Gwen Stefani's first solo album, *Love, Angel, Music, Baby.*

surreal something so strange that it is almost like a dream

Rap stars in films

LL Cool J

Eminem

Ludacris

Will Smith

Tupac Shakur

Ice Cube

Queen Latifah

Snoop Dogg

Movie star

One of Andre's great passions is acting. While making *The Love Below*, he moved to Los Angeles to take acting classes. His first film part was in *Hollywood Homicide* in 2003. The movie starred Harrison Ford and Josh Hartnett as a pair of police detectives. Andre had a small role as a writer named Silk Brown.

Be Cool

Andre's next film was called *Be Cool*. It is a **sequel** to the 1995 film *Get Shorty*. *Be Cool* features a lot of big stars, including John Travolta, Uma Thurman, and the Rock. It came out in 2005.

Andre appeared with Uma Thurman in *Be Cool*.

Star words   director person in charge of making a film

Role as a rapper

The **director** of *Be Cool*, F. Gary Gray, worked on Outkast's video for "Ms. Jackson". He liked working with Andre so much on the video that he created a part in *Be Cool* just for him. Andre is very funny in the movie. He plays a gangsta rapper named Dabu.

More film projects

Andre also hopes one day to play guitar legend Jimi Hendrix in a film. Jimi Hendrix is one of Andre's heroes. He also has the same wild taste in clothes. Andre also features in the **animated film** version of *Charlotte's Web*. He is the voice of Elwyn the crow. Julia Roberts is the voice of Charlotte.

★ ★ ★ ★ ★ ★ ★ ★

Jimi Hendrix

Jimi Hendrix was one of the greatest guitar players of all time. He was famous for playing his guitar behind his head and setting it on fire. Sadly, his **career** was very short. He died of a drug overdose in 1970 when he was just 27.

★ ★ ★ ★ ★ ★

Jimi Hendrix is still very popular today, more than 30 years after his death.

Dressed for success

Andre is almost as famous for his clothes as he is for his music. He makes his own rules when it comes to fashion. Around the time that *Speakerboxxx/The Love Below* came out, Andre changed his look. He began to wear more formal clothes. Andre still adds his own twist. For example, he might wear polka-dot bow ties, bright checkered shirts, and puffy caps.

> To me, that's real style . . . anything that feels comfortable and expresses your personality and makes you stand a little taller.

Rapper wear

Many other people in the rap world have successful clothing lines. Some of the most famous are Phat Farm by Russell Simmons, Wu Wear by the Wu Tang Clan, Sean John by Sean "P. Diddy" Combs, and Rocawear by Jay-Z.

Concert clothing

Andre now saves his wildest outfits for his rare stage performances. At the 2004 NBA All-Star Game he sang "Hey Ya" while dressed as a funky popcorn vendor. Just a few days later, he appeared at the 2004 Brit Awards in a skeleton costume.

Andre takes to the stage at the Brit Awards.

Sly Stone has **influenced** Andre's music and style.

Sly Stone

Sly Stone is one of the founders of funk music. In the 1960s he formed Sly and the Family Stone, one of the first popular groups with both white and black members. Sly sang about unity and equality on such hits as "Everyday People" and "Family Affair".

Outkast Clothing

In 2001 Andre and Big Boi launched the Outkast Clothing Company. They wanted to create clothes that their fans could afford. Outkast clothes were sold in major department stores around the world. Sales reached $20 million in the first year alone. Andre also announced that he wants to launch a clothing line of his own.

Fashion award

In 2004 Andre was named the best-dressed man in the world by *Esquire* magazine in the US. This is a popular men's fashion magazine. Andre ranked ahead of Jude Law, Hugh Grant, and even Prince Charles.

Finding a voice

Andre feels very strongly about voting. "I challenge anybody that's a hip-hop artist who's on the record talking about what's going on in the street and the community: If you haven't voted, you have no right to complain at all."

Choose or lose

In 2004 Andre joined Declare Yourself. This group tries to get Americans to **register** to vote. In the United States anyone who is eighteen or older can vote, but they must register first. In the 2000 presidential election less than 40 percent of young people voted. Andre and other celebrities wanted to make sure that many more young voters turned out for the 2004 election.

Andre talked to voters at the 2004 Democratic Convention in Boston.

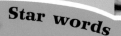
Star words   disrespectful rude

Change of heart

Andre was not sure if he was right for the job. He had actually never voted himself. He soon realized that this made him the perfect person for the job. Andre changed his views on voting. Andre knew that African Americans had fought very hard to earn the right to vote. Some had lost their lives. He believed it was **disrespectful** to them if he did not vote.

Christina Aguilera is one of the many stars who encouraged young people to vote in the 2004 election.

Andre appeared at events around the country. He urged young people to register to vote and let their voices be heard. "If you don't vote, you're pretty much giving up your power," he said. "You're pretty much saying, 'Do what you will with me.'"

Good results

The work of Andre and others paid off. Declare Yourself encouraged more than 1 million Americans to register to vote. More than 20 million young people voted in the presidential election in 2004. This was nearly 5 million more than the number who voted in 2000.

Celebrity voters

Andre is not the only celebrity who was part of Declare Yourself. Other stars who helped sign up young people to vote include Christina Aguilera, Ben Affleck, Tobey Maguire, and Leonardo DiCaprio.

register sign up to vote

The future

★ ★ ★ ★ ★ ★ ★ ★

Famous fans

Many stars of
music and
movies would
love to work
with Andre.
Leonardo
DiCaprio, Reese
Witherspoon,
and Jack White
from the White
Stripes are just
a few of his fans.
Even soul legend
Aretha Franklin
named Outkast
as her favourite
rap group.

★ ★ ★ ★ ★ ★ ★ ★

It is always hard to know what Andre will do next. He has so many projects in the works that it is not clear which one he will tackle first. One thing is for sure: he and Big Boi have not finished making music together.

Only Andre knows what project he will tackle next!

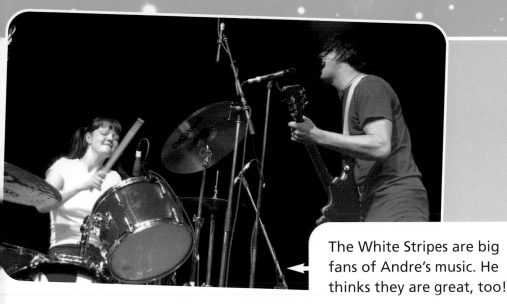

The White Stripes are big fans of Andre's music. He thinks they are great, too!

Outkast returns

In 2005 Outkast released a **soundtrack** to a movie musical. Andre and Big Boi played the lead parts in the film, which also came out in 2005. It is a gangster movie set in the 1930s. Outkast also released another album called *10 the Hard Way*. It was a return to a more **traditional** style of hip-hop and rap.

Early retirement?

Who knows what type of music Andre will turn to next? He has been on top of the music world for more than 10 years. That is a long time for a hip-hop artist. "I don't want to be rapping when I'm 40 years old," Andre says. "Rap is about youth and energy."

Whatever he does, Andre has a healthy view of the future. "Nobody will stay on top forever," he says. "Once you get that in your mind, it won't be such a crash. You just gotta keep on keepin' on."

The future

There are a lot of **rumours** about Andre's future projects. One of them is a film about a wealthy African American man who falls in love with a poor white girl. There are also rumours that Andre and Big Boi are writing a book called *Outkast's Guide to the Galaxy*. Stay tuned to see what Andre does next!

Find out more

Books

One Nation Under a Groove: Rap Music and Its Roots, Jim Haskins (Jump at the Sun, 2000)
Rosa Parks: My Story, Rosa Parks and James Haskins (Puffin Books, 1999)
Black Americans of Achievement: Jimi Hendrix, Sean Piccoli (Chelsea House Publications, 1996)
Avisson Young Adult Series: "I Can Do Anything": The Sammy Davis, Jr. Story, William Schoell (Avisson Press Inc., 2004)

Discography

10 the Hard Way (LaFace Records, 2005)
Speakerboxxx/The Love Below (LaFace Records, 2003)
Big Boi and Dre Present … Outkast (LaFace Records, 2001)
Stankonia (LaFace Records, 2000)
Aquemini (LaFace Records, 1998)
ATLiens (LaFace Records, 1996)
Southernplayalisticadillacmuzik (LaFace Records, 1994)

Filmography

Be Cool (2005)
Revolver (2005)
Hollywood Homicide (2003)

Awards

Grammy Awards (6)

2004: Album of the Year (*Speakerboxxx: The Love Below*)
Best Urban/ Alternative Performance ("Hey Ya")
Best Rap Album (*Speakerboxxx: The Love Below*)

2003: Best Rap Performance by a Duo or Group ("The Whole World" with Killer Mike)

2002: Best Rap Performance by a Duo or Group ("Ms. Jackson")
Best Rap Album (*Stankonia*)

American Music Awards (4)

2004: Favourite Pop/Rock Band/Duo/Group
Favourite Rap Band/Duo/Group
Favourite Album

2003: Favourite Hip-Hop/R&B Band/Duo/Group.

MTV Video Music Awards (5)

2004: (all for "Hey Ya")
Video of the Year
Best Hip-Hop Video
Best Special Effects
Best Art Direction

2001: Best Hip-Hop Video ("Ms. Jackson")

Glossary

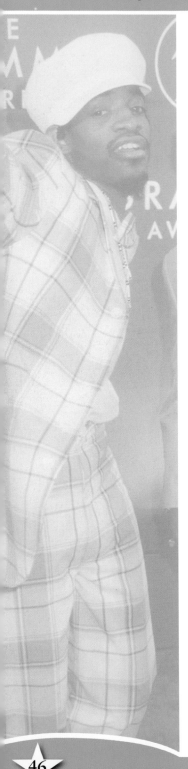

animated film movie that features cartoon characters rather than live actors

argyle pattern with diamond shapes

audition interview for a musician or actor, where they show their skills

blues type of traditional music created by African Americans in the early 1900s

boycott refuse to take part in something to protest against it

career what someone does for a job

category group or class

civil rights movement struggle of African Americans in the 1950s and 1960s to gain the same rights as white people

cliché something that has been overused

deadline due date

debut first

diploma official school document stating that a student has finished his or her studies

director person in charge of making a film

disrespectful rude

downloads files that are copied from the internet onto a computer

dreadlocks long thin mats of hair that have been allowed to grow out over a long period of time without being combed

inducted admitted as a member

influences things that affect our work or actions

inspiration idea that you get from people or things

instrumental song that does not include any singing

mainstream what appeals to most people

manager music managers take care of the business side of a pop star's career

media types of communication such as television, radio, internet, newspapers, and magazines

nominated put forward as one of the right people to win an award

outrageous wild or crazy

performing arts activities such as acting, dance, and music

producer music producers decide how a song will sound when it is being recorded

pronunciation key part of a dictionary entry that tells you how to say the word correctly

rebel act against people in charge

recording contract agreement between an artist and a record label to make music together

register sign up to vote

rumour story that lots of people discuss, but that may not be true

sample part of a recording that is reused by another artist to create a new song

segregate keep one group from another, usually because of race

sequel movie or book that continues an earlier story

soundtrack music in a film

surreal something so strange that it is almost like a dream

theme topic or subject

tradition usual way of doing things

tribute act that shows feelings of respect or admiration toward someone

turban long piece of material wrapped around the head to cover the hair

unique different from everything else

Index